W9-AQV-637

Date: 2/1/12

J 598.33 SEX
Sexton, Colleen A.,
Puffins /

OCEANS ALIVE

Puffins

by Colleen Sexton

BLASTOFF! READERS
2

BELLWETHER MEDIA • MINNEAPOLIS, MN

Note to Librarians, Teachers, and Parents:

Blastoff! Readers are carefully developed by literacy experts and combine standards-based content with developmentally appropriate text.

Level 1 provides the most support through repetition of high-frequency words, light text, predictable sentence patterns, and strong visual support.

Level 2 offers early readers a bit more challenge through varied simple sentences, increased text load, and less repetition of high-frequency words.

Level 3 advances early-fluent readers toward fluency through increased text and concept load, less reliance on visuals, longer sentences, and more literary language.

Level 4 builds reading stamina by providing more text per page, increased use of punctuation, greater variation in sentence patterns, and increasingly challenging vocabulary.

Level 5 encourages children to move from "learning to read" to "reading to learn" by providing even more text, varied writing styles, and less familiar topics.

Whichever book is right for your reader, Blastoff! Readers are the perfect books to build confidence and encourage a love of reading that will last a lifetime!

This edition first published in 2009 by Bellwether Media, Inc.

No part of this publication may be reproduced in whole or in part without written permission of the publisher. For information regarding permission, write to Bellwether Media, Inc., Attention: Permissions Department, Post Office Box 19349, Minneapolis, MN 55419.

Library of Congress Cataloging-in-Publication Data
Sexton, Colleen A., 1967–
 Puffins / by Colleen Sexton.
   p. cm. – (Blastoff! readers. Oceans alive)
 Includes bibliographical references and index.
 Summary: "Simple text and supportive images introduce beginning readers to puffins. Intended for students in kindergarten through third grade"–Provided by publisher.
 ISBN-13: 978-1-60014-251-2 (hardcover : alk. paper)
 ISBN-10: 1-60014-251-6 (hardcover : alk. paper)
 1. Puffins–Juvenile literature. I. Title.

 QL696.C42S49 2009
 598.3'3–dc22   2008033542

Contents

Puffins are **seabirds**.
They fly through the air
and swim in the ocean.

4

Puffins live in the northern half of the world. They spend most of their lives far from land.

bill

webbed feet

Puffins have large **bills** and **webbed feet**.

Their bills and feet are bright colors in summer. The colors are dull the rest of the year.

Puffins have thick bodies with powerful muscles.

Puffins have short wings.

Puffin feathers trap air to keep puffins warm and help them float.

Trapped air helps a puffin swim or float. Puffins push out the air when they are ready to dive.

Puffins can dive about
100 feet (30 meters) deep.

They flap their wings to swim.
They **steer** with their feet.

Puffins dive to catch fish, **squid**, and other sea animals.

Puffins stay underwater for
about a minute. Then they
must come up for air.

Puffins fly to land in the spring. They gather together in **colonies** to nest.

Each puffin finds its **mate**.
The two puffins meet in the
same place every year.

The female puffin lays one egg in a **burrow**. A chick hatches six weeks later.

The male and female
take turns finding food
for their hungry chick.

19

The puffin flies out to sea and brings back a mouthful of fish.

A puffin can carry as many as 20 small fish at once!

Glossary

bill—the hard mouth of a bird

burrow—a hole in the ground where animals live or make their nests

colony—a large group of animals that live together; puffin colonies nest on rocky islands and shores.

mate—one of a pair of animals that have young together

seabird—a type of bird that lives much of its life in the ocean far away from land

squid—an ocean animal with a long body, eight arms, and two tentacles; puffins eat small squids.

steer—to guide in a certain direction

webbed feet—feet with thin skin between the toes

To Learn More

AT THE LIBRARY

Kress, Stephen W. *Project Puffin: How We Brought Puffins Back to Egg Rock*. Gardiner, Maine: Tilbury House, 1997.

McMillan, Bruce. *Puffins Climb, Penguins Rhyme*. San Diego, Calif.: Harcourt Brace, 2001.

Squire, Ann O. *Puffins*. New York: Children's Press, 2007.

ON THE WEB

Learning more about puffins is as easy as 1, 2, 3.

1. Go to www.factsurfer.com.

2. Enter "puffins" into the search box.

3. Click the "Surf" button and you will see a list of related Web sites.

With factsurfer.com, finding more information is just a click away.

Index

The images in this book are reproduced through the courtesy of: Thomas O'Neil, front cover; Ian Jeffery, p. 4; Juan Martinez, p. 5; Michael Melford, p. 6; Barbara Gerlach, p. 7; Dennis Donohue, pp. 8-9; John Butterfield, p. 10; Photoshot Holdings Ltd / Alamy, p. 11; Chris Gomersall / Alamy, pp. 12-13; Art Wolfe, p. 14; Bpperry, p. 15; Jeremy Woodhouse / Masterfile, pp. 16-17; Getty Images, pp. 18, 20; Lisbeth Landstrom, p. 19; Andrew Parkinson, p. 21.